BASIC/NOT BORING
LANGUAGE SKILLS

SPELLING

Grades 4-5

Inventive Exercises to Sharpen
Skills and Raise Achievement

Series Concept & Development
by Imogene Forte & Marjorie Frank

Exercises by Majorie Frank

Illustrations by Kathleen Bullock

Incentive Publications, Inc.
Nashville, Tennessee

About the cover:

Bound resist, or tie dye, is the most ancient known method of fabric surface design. The brilliance of the basic tie dye design on this cover reflects the possibilities that emerge from the mastery of basic skills.

Cover art by Mary Patricia Deprez, dba Tye Dye Mary®
Cover design by Marta Drayton, Joe Shibley, and W. Paul Nance
Edited by Jennifer E. Janke

ISBN 0-86530-432-7

PRINTED IN THE UNITED STATES OF AMERICA

TABLE OF CONTENTS

CELEBRATE BASIC LANGUAGE SKILLS

Basic does not mean boring! There certainly is nothing dull about . . .

   . . . tracking down misspelled words with a famous detective, a clever magician, a dragon-fighting knight, a daring skydiver, an adventuresome scuba diver, a charming snake charmer, a tough Wild West sheriff, and a quartet of queens in quicksand!

   . . . finding out where molasses, mosquitoes, and doughnuts came from

   . . . having success spelling foods, cities, funny words, and people's quirks

   . . . showing off by spelling "mouthful" words like electromagnetic and abracadabra

   . . . mastering tricky words loaded with Os, Qs, Ws, Ss, Ys, and Zs

   . . . getting control over that devious duo that mess up so many words: i and e

   . . . tackling troublesome words and getting the better of them

   . . . learning when to let letters be silent and when to let them speak

   . . . cleaning up outrageously misspelled words, headlines, and titles

The idea of celebrating the basics is just what it sounds like—enjoying and getting good at the basic skills of spelling. The pages that follow are full of exercises for students that will help to review and strengthen specific skills in the content area of language arts. But this is not just any ordinary fill-in-the-blanks way to learn. These activities are interesting, surprising, and useful. Students are led through the pages by a delightful cast of frogs who encourage them to focus on and apply the most important skills of spelling: improving spelling accuracy and getting good at eradicating misspellings.

The pages in this book can be used in many ways:
- for individual students to sharpen or practice a skill
- with a small group needing to re-learn or sharpen a skill
- as an instructional tool for teaching a skill to any size group
- by students working on their own
- by students working under the direction of a parent or teacher

Each page may be used to introduce a new skill, reinforce a skill, or assess a student's ability to perform a skill. However students use these pages, as they take on the challenges of these adventures with words, you'll see that they are growing in their mastery of spelling, and having a good time while they're doing it. And as you watch them check off the basic spelling skills they've sharpened, you can celebrate with them!

The Skills Test

Use the skills test beginning on page 56 as a pretest and/or a post-test. This will help you check the students' mastery of spelling skills and will prepare them for success on achievement tests.

SKILLS CHECKLIST FOR
SPELLING, Grades 4-5

✔	SKILL	PAGE(S)
	Correctly spell words with double consonants	10
	Identify words that are spelled incorrectly	10, 13, 15, 23, 33, 35, 37, 40, 43, 48
	Correctly spell words that use the *ie* rules	11
	Identify words that are spelled correctly	11, 12, 18, 25, 28, 36, 46, 47
	Correctly spell compound words	12
	Correctly spell words with confusing initial consonant sounds and blends	13
	Follow rules to spell plural nouns correctly	14
	Correctly spell commonly-used proper nouns	15
	Follow rules to form past tense of verbs	16
	Choose the correct ending for a specific word	17–21
	Distinguish among similar endings	17–21
	Correctly spell words that break the rules	22
	Use knowledge of roots to spell words correctly	23
	Correctly spell words with prefixes	24
	Correctly spell words with suffixes	25
	Spell words that contain silent letters	26
	Correctly spell words that contain special letters: *q, s, w, x, y, z*	27–32
	Correctly spell words that contain the letter *o*	33
	Correctly spell words with special vowel combinations	34
	Correctly spell very difficult or unusual words	35
	Correctly spell and distinguish among words that look or sound similar	36
	Correctly spell and distinguish among homophones	37
	Correctly spell words of foreign origin	38
	Correctly spell words that fall into a variety of categories	39–41, 44, 45
	Correctly spell small words	42
	Correctly spell big words	43
	Correctly spell commonly misspelled words	46
	Use knowledge of spelling to edit brief passages	49, 50

SPELLING

Skills Exercises

DOUBLE TROUBLE

Freddy Frog can never quite get his binoculars adjusted right. So, he sees everything double.
Today, he sees double consonants in all of these words. Some of them really do have double
letters. Some of them should not! Which ones are right?

Read all the words that Freddy is seeing. Circle each word that is
NOT spelled correctly.

annimal   glossary   balloon   commit

community   impress   bennefit   memmory

Tennessee   opposite   proffessor   marshmallow

necessary   flammable   scissors   tommorrow

accent   accident   address   different   catterpillar

vollunteer   suppose   horrid   struggle

misspell   accuse   baskettball   bannanna   buffalo

tellescope

attenndance   difference   illegal   irregular

terrible   immune   issue   lasso   dessert

Name

A TROUBLESOME TWOSOME

Freida and Fiefie are the most mischievous frogs around. Since they are cousins, everyone always gets them confused with one another. Notice that one has a name with *i* before *e*. The other has a name with *e* before *i*. Do you remember the *ie* rule?

Use the *ie* rule to clear up the trouble with these words below. Choose the correct spelling for each word.

1. a. grief
   b. greif

2. a. retreive
   b. retrieve

3. a. cheif
   b. chief

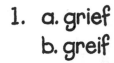
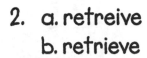

Wheeeeeeeeee

You go, girl!

4. a. freind
   b. friend

5. a. neighbor
   b. nieghbor

6. a. receipt
   b. reciept

7. a. eighty
   b. ieghty

8. a. sleigh
   b. sliegh

9. a. ceiling
   b. cieling

10. a. riendeer
    b. reindeer

11. a. believe
    b. beleive

12. a. riegn
    b. reign

13. a. veil
    b. viel

14. a. receive
    b. recieve

15. a. freight
    b. frieght

16. a. biege
    b. beige

17. a. weight
    b. wieght

18. a. decieve
    b. deceive

Name

11   *Basic Skills/Spelling 4-5*

WORDS THAT STICK TOGETHER

Oops! Freddy spilled the glue all over his spelling homework. Lots of the words got stuck together. That's okay, because pairs of words have been made into compound words. The problem is, some of the compound words are spelled correctly, while others are all wrong. Use crayons or markers to color the sticky papers that have compound words SPELLED CORRECTLY.

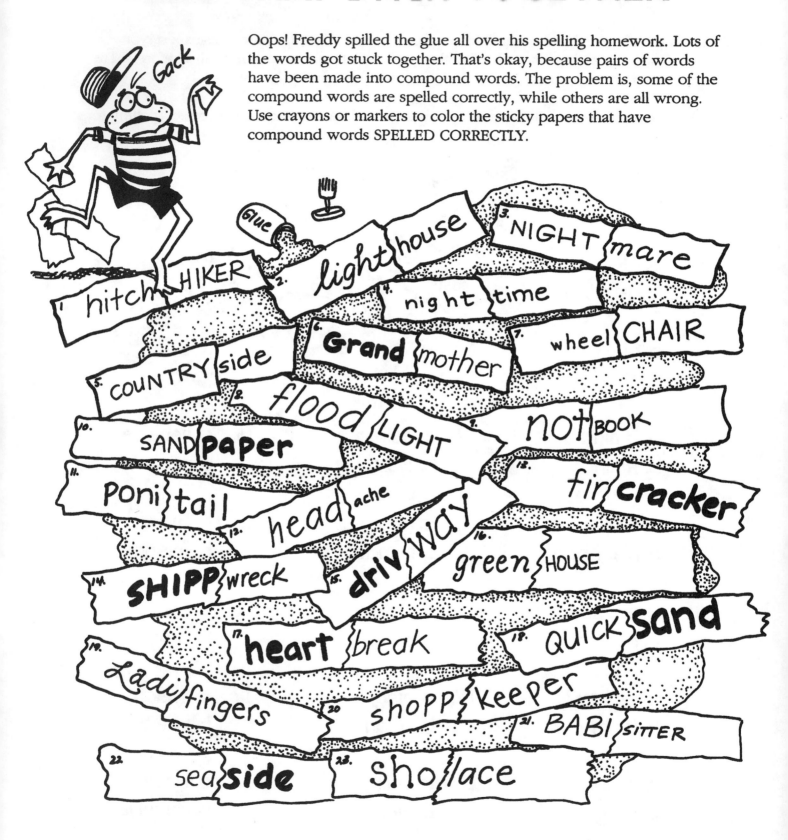

1. hitch HIKER
2. light house
3. NIGHT mare
4. night time
5. COUNTRY side
6. Grand mother
7. wheel CHAIR
8. flood LIGHT
9. not BOOK
10. SAND paper
11. poni tail
12. head ache
13. fir cracker
14. SHIPP wreck
15. driv way
16. green HOUSE
17. heart break
18. QUICK sand
19. Lady fingers
20. shopp keeper
21. BABI sitter
22. sea side
23. sho lace

Name

LETTERS WITH A SECRET LIFE

Some letters are rather sneaky. The letter *c* can sound like a *k* or an *s*. And *s* sometimes sounds like *z*. Sometimes *g* sounds hard. Other times it sounds soft like a *j*. Then, there's those mysterious pairs, *gh* and *ph*. They often sound like *f*!

In her secret diary, Phoebe Phrog uses many words with these letters. See if you can find the mistakes in her diary entries! Circle any misspelled words. Then write them correctly on the lines below each entry.

Friday, June 13

What an unlucky day! At the circis, I was cheering and laffing and eating at the same time. I choked on a piece of selery, and had to be taken to the emerjensy room. Finally, I couffed up the selery. My throat is still sore.

_____

_____

_____

Saturday, June 14

Today, I got a fone call from a foney juge. He was asking me to take a sitisenship test. Isn't that ridikulous?

_____

_____

_____

Sunday, June 15

Two gastly gosts crashed my birthday selebation today. They caused much mischeph and drank up all the sider.

_____

_____

Monday, June 16

After my fizical fitness class today, I was sertainly energised. They surprized me by taking fotografs of my fifty-three pushups.

_____

_____

_____

Tuesday, June 17

I got caut in a syclone today. Afterwards, I had no patiense left to go to my skuba lesson.

_____

_____

_____

Name _____

TOO MANY FROGS

Freida never should have taken this babysitting job! There are just too many little frogs to watch at once! In fact, she's decided that more than one frog is too many!

All these words name ONE of something. How would you write them if they named MORE THAN ONE? Write the plural form of each word. Spell each one correctly!

1. child _____
2. noise _____
3. mess _____
4. wish _____
5. society _____
6. cottage _____
7. address _____
8. chef _____

9. butterfly _____
10. hero _____
11. loaf _____
12. chief _____
13. goose _____
14. echo _____
15. donkey _____

16. woman _____
17. radio _____
18. key _____
19. potato _____
20. athlete _____

21. lunch _____
22. fox _____
23. county _____
24. nest _____
25. attorney _____

Name _____

14

TO NAME A FEW

Phantom Frog, the mysterious superhero, has stopped disasters and saved lives all over the world. This is Phantom Frog's list of the places he's gone to work in the past month. Unfortunately, Phantom is a rather poor speller. Fix the spelling on his list. Cross out any misspelled words and rewrite them correctly!

PHANTOM FROG'S RESCUE LIST

1. Ejipt
2. North Atlantac Ocen
3. Las Angelas
4. The Iffle Tower
5. Innerstate 80
6. Quene Elizabeth's Kichen
7. The Goldan Gate Brige
8. Detroit, Misshigan
9. Jupitar
10. Mounte Rushmore
11. Warshington D.C.
12. The Phillippinnes
13. The Statu of Libertie
14. The Amizon River
15. Anarctica
16. Rode Island
17. South Amerika
18. Parris, France
19. Australea
20. Brasil

Name

OUT OF THE PAST

Meet Sir Felix Frog, the brave knight right out of the Middle Ages. Read the phrases about his activities. Since he lived long ago, each verb must be used in the past tense. Write each verb to show that the action happened in the past. Make sure you spell them all correctly.

1. (fight) _____ dragons every day

2. never (argue) _____ with the king

3. only (giggle) _____ in private

4. job (require) _____ much courage

5. (choose) _____ to live in the castle

6. (polish) _____ his sword every night

7. always (bring) _____ gifts to the king

8. was not (worry) _____ about any battles

9. feet (get) _____ blisters from the heavy armor

10. never (marry) _____ the girl of his dreams

11. toes (freeze) _____ on one long winter trip

12. once (shine) _____ his sword with bear fur

13. suit of armor (rust) _____ when he (forget)

 _____ to dry it off

14. (try) _____ for years to train his horse to

bow to the king

15. secretly (wish) _____ he could be

a court jester

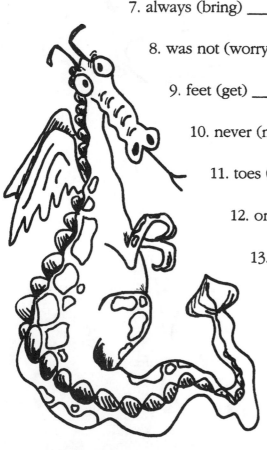

Name _____

16

THE CASE OF THE VANISHING ENDINGS

Famous Detective Sherlock Frog is searching for the endings that are missing from these words. Help him track them down. Write the correct ending for each word.

1. favor _____

2. negat _____

3. surpr _____

4. self _____

5. varn _____

6. critic _____

7. fool _____

8. prom _____

9. expens _____

10. dent _____

11. frag _____

12. apolog _____

13. van _____

14. host _____

15. coll _____

16. knowl _____

17. man _____

18. flor _____

19. garb _____

20. cour _____

It's a clue!

ise   ish

ege   ize   ite   ive

ile   ist   age   edge

Name

TRICKY ENDINGS

Mannifrog the Magnificent is the most respected frog magician in the land. He does the most awesome tricks and pulls the most amazing things out of his hat!

The endings coming out of Mannifrog's hat are tricky ones. They often confuse even the best spellers. For each word below, choose the tricky ending that is the right one. Circle the word with the ending that makes the correct spelling.

1. jealous
   jealus
   jealius
   jealeous

2. circous
   circus
   circeus
   circius

3. focous
   foceous
   focus
   foceus

4. tremendus
   tremendeous
   tremendous
   tremendious

5. melodus
   melodious
   melodeous
   melodius

6. generus
   generius
   generous
   generuous

7. marvelus
   marvelous
   marveleous
   marvious

8. conscious
   conscius
   consceous
   coinscius

9. cautious
   cauteous
   cautus
   cuteous

10. radeous
    radeus
    radius
    radious

11. outrageus
    outragius
    outrageous
    outragous

12. luscious
    lusceous
    luscus
    luscius

13. Venus
    Venuous
    Venous
    Veneus

14. nerveous
    nervus
    nervous
    nervious

15. cacteous
    cactus
    cactuous
    cactius

Name _____

ANTS FOR SALE

On weekends, Freddy operates the Frogville Sweet Shop, where he sells yummy chocolate covered ants, minted flies, caramel grasshoppers, and other tasty delights. Many of the candies contain ants.

Many of these words contain ants also. Which ones end with *ant*? Which ones end with *ent*, *int*, *ence*, or *ance*? Choose the correct ending for each word.

WRITE THE WHOLE WORD!

1. dist (ant, ent, int) _____

2. evid (ant, ent, int) _____

3. hydr (ant, ent, int) _____

4. independ (ant, ent, int) _____

5. pleas (ant, ent, int) _____

6. eleg (ant, ent, int) _____

7. vac (ant, ent, int) _____

8. excitem (ant, ent, int) _____

9. ignor (ant, ent, int) _____

10. import (ence, ance) _____

11. appli (ence, ance) _____

12. eleph (ant, ent, int) _____

13. restaur (ant, ent, int) _____

14. sci (ence, ance) _____

15. abs (ence, ance) _____

16. insur (ence, ance) _____

17. attend (ence, ance) _____

18. evid (ence, ance) _____

Name _____

TANGLED ENDINGS

Frieda is the top forecaster for Frogville's Weather Channel 10. She predicted this violent whirl-wind. Now she's out there, reporting live from the scene of the storm.

Notice that the whirlwind has made a mess of these words. It has mixed up all the endings.

Untangle these endings. Find the correct ending for each word. Cross out the wrong ending and write the correct one above it to spell the word right.

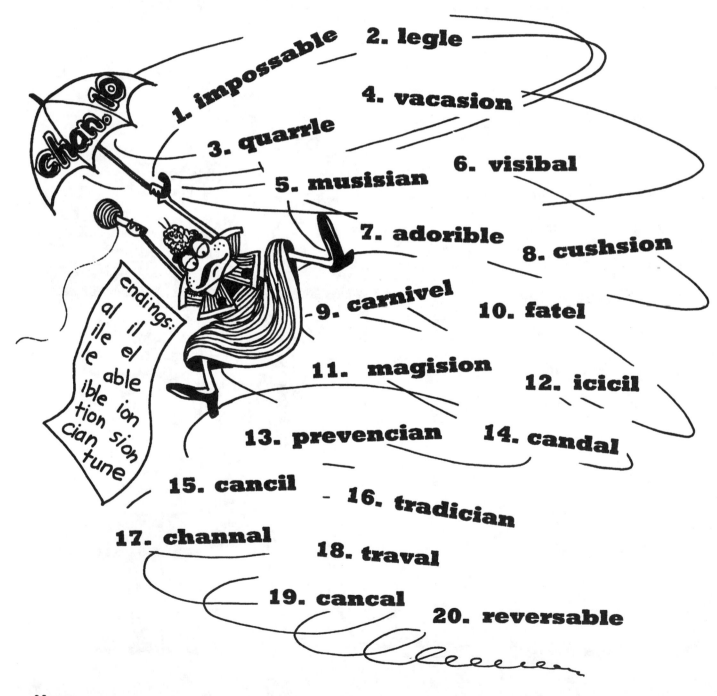

1. impossable
2. legle
3. quarrle
4. vacasion
5. musisian
6. visibal
7. adorible
8. cushsion
9. carnivel
10. fatel
11. magision
12. icicil
13. prevencian
14. candal
15. cancil
16. tradician
17. channal
18. traval
19. cancal
20. reversable

endings:
al   il
ile   el
le   able
ible ion
tion sion
cian tune

Name _____

YOU ATE THAT?

EAT and ATE are built right into many words. Some of them are good for eating. Some are not. Alexanderia Amphibian ate them all. Now she's sorry!

Decide what the correct ending is for each of these words. Choose from these four endings.

1. chocol _____

2. accur _____

3. rot _____

4. retr _____

5. imit _____

6. loc _____

7. del _____

8. celebr _____

9. favor _____

10. gradu _____

11. educ _____

12. def _____

13. decor _____

14. hibern _____

15. compl _____

16. separ _____

17. candid _____

18. defin _____

Name _____

RULE-BREAKERS

Some words just don't follow the spelling rules. Instead,
they break the rules!

Read each rule. Then look at the group of words which
follows it. Circle every word that BREAKS the rule.

RULE # 1
When a word ends in **o**, and there is a consonant
before the **o**, make the word plural by adding **es**.

tomatoes   **torpedoes**   **pianos**   **volcanoes**   **potatoes**   **solos**

RULE # 2
i comes before **e**, except after **c** or when sounding like **a** as in *neighbor* or *weigh*.

weird   **beige**   **chief**   **receive**   **ancient**   **neither**
height   **their**   **foreign**

RULE # 3
When two words join to become a **compound** word, the spelling of each part of
the new compound word stays the same as the spelling of each word before
being joined.

roommate   **pastime**   **sandpaper**   **homework**   **bookkeeper**

RULE # 4
When **ly** is added to the root, the spelling of the root word does not change,
unless the root ends in **y**.

beautifully   **wholly**   **lately**   **truly**   **friendly**   **lovely**

RULE # 5
When a root ends in **e**, drop the **e** before adding a suffix that begins with a vowel
(such as *ate, ous, able, y, ate*).

hoping   **noticeable**   **shiny**   **famous**   **manageable**

Name _____

AT THE ROOT OF IT ALL

When you need to spell a word with a prefix or suffix, it helps to think about the root. Get the root's spelling right, and you're well on your way to the correct spelling of the whole word.

Use your knowledge of roots to help you find the errors in these words. If a word is spelled wrong, write it correctly on the lines at the bottom of the page.

1. supernatral

2. accidental

3. export

4. suspend

5. completly

6. fevorish

7. difference

8. prefer

9. frequently

10. biograffy

11. magecal

12. disapear

13. preskool

14. selfish

15. toothless

16. musacal

17. unlock

18. favorable

19. imperfect

20. advertizement

Finally! We've gotten to the ROOT of the matter!

gulp

voila!

Name _____

ADDITIONS TO THE BEGINNING

Thousands of words have little word parts added to their beginnings. If you know how to spell these prefixes, you'll have a good start on correct spelling of the whole word!

These frogmen make a lot of use of a prefix that means "under."
Use your knowledge of prefixes to spell these words right.
Write a word to match each clue.

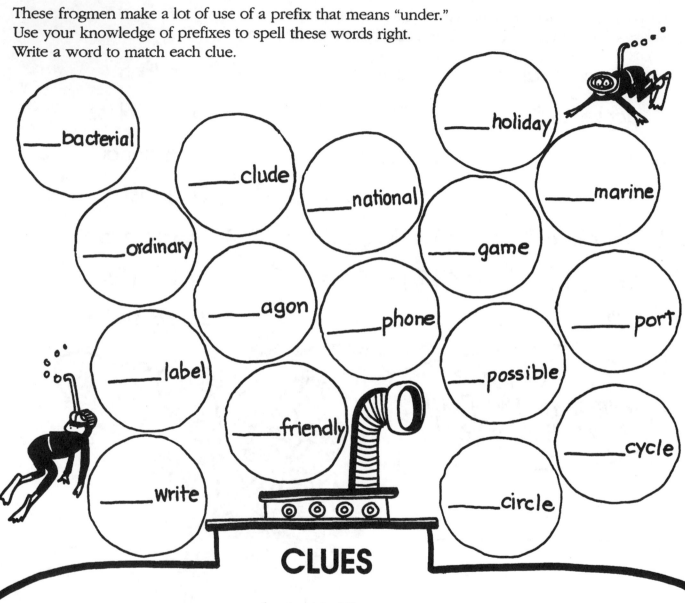

_____bacterial

_____clude

_____national

_____holiday

_____marine

_____ordinary

_____game

_____agon

_____phone

_____port

_____label

_____possible

_____friendly

_____cycle

_____write

_____circle

CLUES

1. under the ocean
2. a tiny phone
3. beyond the ordinary
4. to write again
5. a cycle with one wheel
6. six-sided figure
7. not possible
8. between nations
9. label something wrong
10. carry something across
11. to leave out
12. before the game
13. after the holidays
14. against bacteria
15. half of a circle
16. not friendly

Name

ADDITIONS TO THE END

Phoebe's hope (see picture) is made possible by some of those little word parts called suffixes. If you know how to spell suffixes, you'll have a better chance at ending up with the correct spelling of the whole word!

Color the parachutes that have words spelled correctly. Pay special attention to those suffixes.

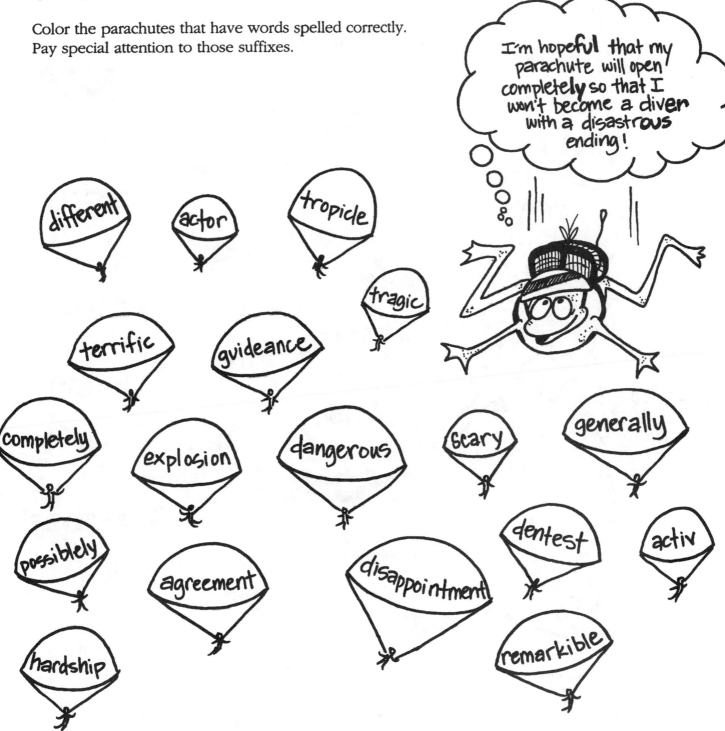

Name _____

LAZY LETTERS

Some letters fall asleep on the job, and make no sound **at all**! You stay awake and investigate these words. Look and listen to find the silent letters.
Draw a path for the sleepwalker by joining words that have silent letters. The path should only touch words with silent letters.

sleepwalker

stalk

KNOT

envy

rhyme

dough

character

resign

ghost

burglar

knife

examine

universe

bumpy

bridge

knee   quiver

COCONUT

designer

combing

automatic

reign

honest

wrote

erupt

wriggle

SWORD

Name

QUARTETS, QUICKSAND, & QUEENS

Find a Q word to match each clue. (The word will have a *q* in it!)
Write the word.
Spell it correctly!

1. unusual   u __ __ qu __

2. ask   i __ qu __ __ __

3. take over   c __ __ qu __

4. smash   __ qu __ sh

5. feast   b __ __ qu __

6. line around
   Earth's middle   __ qu __ __ __ r

7. in a hurry   qu __ __ __ ly

8. not noisy   qu __ __ __

9. follow-up
   story   s __ qu __ l

10. heavy
    blanket   qu __ __ __

11. four singers qu __ __ t __ __

12. tests   qu __ z __ __ __

13. fish tank   __ qu __ __ __ __ m

14. argue   qu __ __ __ __ l

15. often   __ __ __ qu __ __ __ ly

16. to ask   qu __ __ t __ __ __

17. tools   __ qu __ __ __ ent

QUIXOTIC

Uh oh

A quartet of quirky queens in the quicksand.

Name _____

SURPRISING S

S is a wonderful letter. It sneaks and sizzles, spies and snoozes.

What is the correct way to spell these words that are homes to the letter S? Use a colored marker to circle the words that are spelled correctly.

1. slippery
2. squerm
3. straght
4. suspec
5. serius
6. soccer
7. spinich
8. stomach
9. saveings
10. susage
11. suspect
12. satasfy
13. sombody
14. serious
15. stereo
16. sneek
17. silance
18. smothe
19. scarcly
20. sammwich
21. secretery
22. seventh
23. strengthen
24. scissors
25. hissing
26. surely
27. successful
28. sosiety
29. special
30. seize
31. squirm
32. studio

Name

WHO'S GONE WRONG?

Sheriff Wilbur Wise Walfrog has just posted the pictures of all the scoundrels WANTED in Frogville for doing something WRONG.

He has some trouble with his spelling. Please write the names correctly under each picture.

William Waitlifter   Retched Ray   Werst Wodepecker

Weird Wanda Werm   Wressler Rachel   Weekend Warriar

Find the mistakes in these words. Write each word correctly.

1. aweful _____   9. knowlege _____

2. waistful _____   10. wreeth _____

3. windowsil _____   11. wispher _____

4. wieght _____   12. wraping _____

5. wunderful _____   13. whiped _____

6. wepons _____   14. Wenesday _____

7. wich _____   15. rinkled _____

8. wer'e _____   16. weekness _____

Name _____

EXTRAORDINARY WORDS

When Casey Frog comes to bat, the fans have high expectations! They cheer and shout out a lot of words that contain *X*!

This word puzzle contains at least 25 words that contain *X*.
Use the clues to help you find the words (horizontal or vertical).
Circle the words if they are spelled correctly.

```
E X P E C T R E X P E L L M O X I e E
G O X E U S A X O P H O N E L I T T
e X T I N C T P R E F L E X B L A X
M E E X C E L L E N T E X I S T X P
H M X G G N R O N P E E X C L A I M
H A A J X E W D E E K F F O X E S I
e X M C C X Y E X C I T I N G P P X
X I I C C T M N E X T I N C T O O T
A M N O D S L Q R E X T R E M E K U
G U E X P R E S S W A Y E E E T L R
O M J Y W E Z Z K F L E X I B L E E
N R W G E X C U S E K K A B O X E S
E O M E P I F F E X E R C I S E H H
M D S N O T X L K E E X T E R I O R
```

Excellent!

Exceptional!

Extraordinary!

1. throw out of school
2. musical instrument
3. species no longer alive
4. country south of USA
5. tighten a muscle
6. absolutely great
7. look at closely
8. to be
9. a six-sided figure
10. the greatest amount
11. shout
12. thrilling
13. what comes after this
14. animals with bushy tails
15. severe
16. gas needed for life
17. reason for something
18. moving the body
19. the outside
20. bendable
21. stuff stirred together
22. go out
23. know something will happen
24. burst or blow up
25. freeway

Name _____

WILY WORDS

The word wily means tricky or slippery! Many words with *y* are tricky to spell. Sometimes it's tough to figure out where the *y* belongs in the word!

Use the clues to help you unscramble these words. Make sure you spell them right!

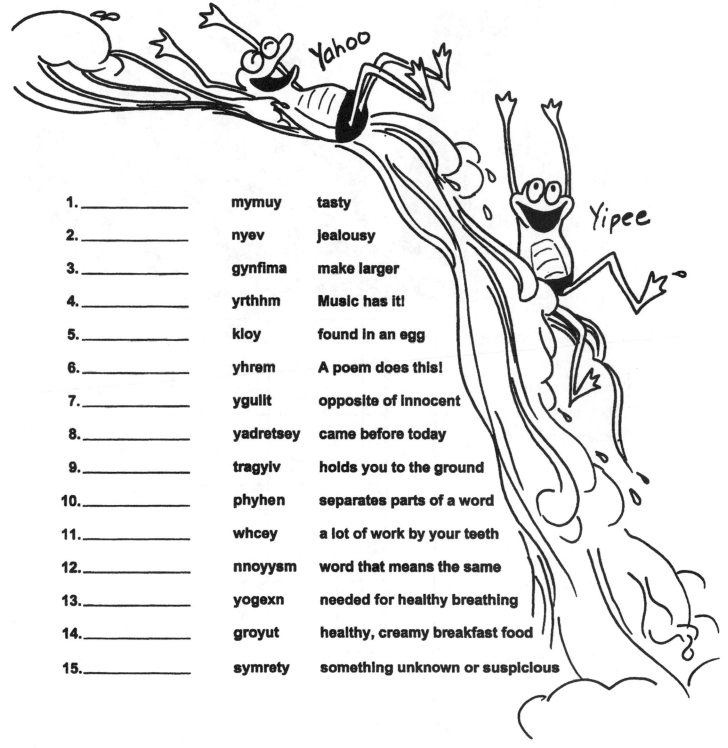

#	scrambled	clue
1. _____	mymuy	tasty
2. _____	nyev	jealousy
3. _____	gynfima	make larger
4. _____	yrthhm	Music has it!
5. _____	kloy	found in an egg
6. _____	yhrem	A poem does this!
7. _____	ygulit	opposite of innocent
8. _____	yadretsey	came before today
9. _____	tragyiv	holds you to the ground
10. _____	phyhen	separates parts of a word
11. _____	whcey	a lot of work by your teeth
12. _____	nnoyysm	word that means the same
13. _____	yogexn	needed for healthy breathing
14. _____	groyut	healthy, creamy breakfast food
15. _____	symrety	something unknown or suspicious

Name _____

WORDS WITH PIZZAZ

The letter Z puts pizzaz into words. (That means sparkle and excitement!) Use correctly-spelled words with z to finish the puzzle below!

ACROSS

1. trophy
3. closes up your jacket
5. flies do this in your ear
7. say you're sorry
9. place to keep ice cream
11. amount equal to nothing
13. severe snowstorm
16. to slowly burn out
17. a kind of music
18. comfortable and warm

DOWN

2. get things in order
4. hug
6. dangerous situation
8. twelve of something
10. figure something out
12. not working hard
14. wobbly from spinning
15. full of bubbles

Name _____

THE OUTSTANDING, OUTRAGEOUS O

Os show up lots of places in words: in the beginning, in the middle, or at the end! Ophelia Phrog, the famous opera singer, warms up her voice by singing a lot of Oooooooooooooos.

Find the words with mistakes. Write each one correctly next to the misspelled word .

1. trio _____

2. carret _____

3. studio _____

4. pilat _____

5. molacule _____

6. volcono _____
7. people _____
8. docter _____
9. oppisite _____
10. memary _____

11. gerilla _____
12. octapus _____
13. Octobor _____
14. kazoo _____
15. scorpian _____

16. cacoon _____
17. shampoo _____
18. masquito _____
19. abdamen _____
20. dinasaur _____

21. lasso _____
22. ooze _____
23. oder _____
24. foolish _____
25. goon _____

Name _____

WINNING COMBINATIONS

Cousins Francine and Flossie are a winning combination on the tennis court. They always get the right score in their doubles matches.

See if you can get a perfect score by finding the winning vowel combinations for each of the words below.

1. app____r
2. thr____gh
3. str____ght

4. r____ned
5. f____ght
6. n____ghty

7. ag____n
8. f____ntain
9. dr____d
10. n____sy
11. cl____

12. excl____m
13. p____ple
14. aud____nce
15. ann____nce
16. c____ght

17. wr____th
18. us____l
19. t____ght
20. be____ty

ea ua eo
au oa ie ai ou ue ui oi

Name _____

PECULIAR WORDS

Dr. Frogenstein is very proud of the very peculiar creature he has created. He also enjoys collecting peculiar words. But he is never quite sure how to spell them!

Check out each word in Dr. Frogenstein's collection. Circle the words that are spelled correctly. If a word is not spelled correctly, cross it out, and write the correct spelling nearby.

Speak, oh monster of mine . . . . .

RIBBIT

bizarre

kazoo

opaque

gnome

moustache

enough

ziggzagg

unique

scheme

De Moines

vacum

neumonia

vague

lama

toung

Conneticut

bronkitis

bough

karate

amnesia

Name

LOOK-ALIKE WORDS

Is Freddy, the hot air balloonist, checking out his attitude or his altitude?
He needs to know the difference between the two words in order to be sure!

Be careful with the spelling of words that look a lot like each other.
Color the puzzle parts that contain words used (and spelled) correctly.

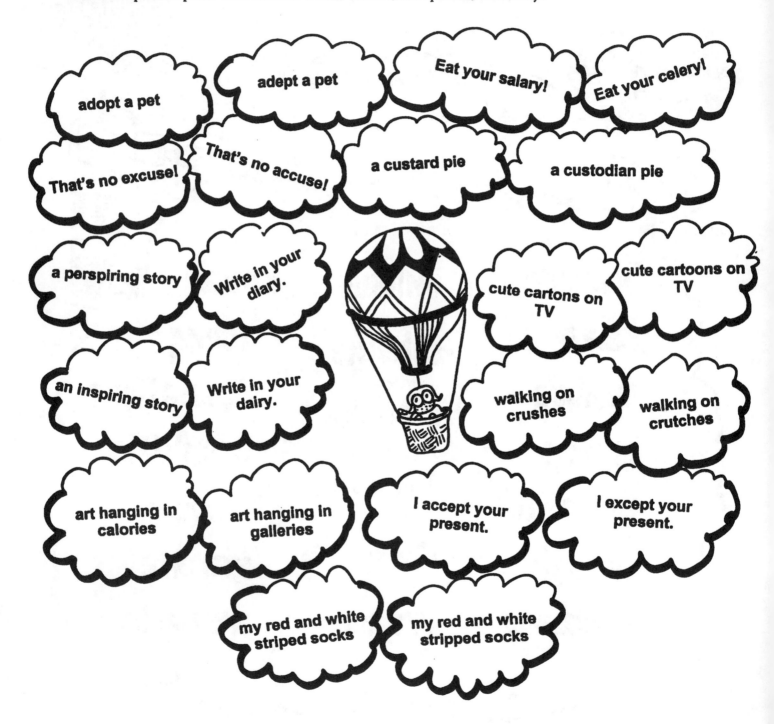

adopt a pet

adept a pet

Eat your salary!

Eat your celery!

That's no excuse!

That's no accuse!

a custard pie

a custodian pie

a perspiring story

Write in your diary.

cute cartons on TV

cute cartoons on TV

an inspiring story

Write in your dairy.

walking on crushes

walking on crutches

art hanging in calories

art hanging in galleries

I accept your present.

I except your present.

my red and white striped socks

my red and white striped socks

Name

36

SOUND-ALIKE WORDS

Does the music sound **suite** or **sweet**?
Are they singing a **ballad** or a **ballot**?
At the end of the performance, will the
singers take a **bough** or a **bow**?

Watch out for words that sound alike
(homonyms)! Don't get the wrong word
for the wrong spot!

Look for the wrong spellings in these
sentences. If you find a misspelled word,
write it correctly at the end of the sentence.
(There might be more than one in a sentence.)

1. Who pride open this can of fudge? _____

2. Are your bones getting
   old and creeky? _____

3. I can't weight to see
   who wins the gold metal! _____

4. The king decided to leave his thrown
   after he had rained for forty years. _____

5. Mom scent her away from the table
   because she choose her food too loudly. _____

6. "Stay indoors tonight," Mother Rat warned her
   children. "You don't want to frees your tales!" _____

7. My ant's boss gave her
   a 10 percent rays. _____

8. Oh no! My library books
   have been overdo for a weak! _____

9. After the concert, all the
   singers' voices were a little horse. _____

10. My dog let out a hoop when
    he caught the cent of the skunk. _____

11. Instead of milk and cookies, I left
    milk and serial for Santa Claws. _____

12. Petal your bike hard, or you'll get
    to school after the bell has wrung. _____

13. The fleece are bothering our dog.
    Maybe we should cut off his hare. _____

Name _____

BORROWED WORDS

Some of the most wonderful words in the English language are not really English! They have been borrowed from other languages, but they add interest and flavor to ours.

Professor Froglegs has written some borrowed words on the chalkboard for his students. But the professor has a bit of a spelling problem. He has them all wrong!

Write the words correctly to match their meanings.

BORROWED WORDS

commet	(Greek)	dimond	(Greek)
moskitoe	(Spanish)	lassoo	(Spanish)
pianoe	(Italian)	doenut	(Latin)
antike	(French)	dinamyte	(Greek)
pirat	(Latin)	octapus	(Latin)
tornadoe	(Spanish)	pygamas	(Indian)
spagetti	(Italian)	kindergarden	(German)
shamppo	(Indian)	vannilla	(Spanish)
yaht	(Dutch)	umbrela	(Italian)

1. long pasta _____

2. breakfast pastry _____

3. pesky insect _____

4. pre-school _____

5. large boat _____

6. night-time clothing _____

7. robber at sea _____

8. 8-legged sea creature _____

9. rain protection _____

10. soap for hair _____

11. flavoring _____

12. burning streak in sky _____

13. cowboy's rope _____

14. music maker _____

15. old and valuable _____

16. explosive _____

17. valuable gem _____

18. funnel-shaped storm _____

Name _____

WORDS YOU CAN EAT

Famous Chef Pierre LaFrog serves wonderful delights at his Chez Froggie Café. Frogs who come there to dine can choose from several menus.

Read these menus carefully. Use a crayon or marker to color the menus with all the words spelled correctly. For the other menus, count the number of words spelled wrong. Write the number next to each menu.

1
bacon quiche
vegtable stew
strawberries
anchovy dip
mollasses pie

2
shrimp appetisers
artichoke butter
cocanut ice cream
diet soda
apple crum pie

3
cranberrys
spinuch salid
cucumber slices
suger cookies
brocoli tips

4
sausage balls
mushroom salad
macaroni & cheese
mustard dip
hamburger

5
fresh pastta
lam casserole
celary sticks
pinapple
bolloney sandwich

6
coconut
noodles
salmon cakes
raddishes
onion soup

7
cabbage
lettuce
custard
cinnamon cakes
cheesecake

8
cheeze biscits
appricot jam
bean burritos
chocalate sunday
bannana cream pie

We never serve frog's legs at the Chez Froggie Café!

Kiss the Chef

Name

WORDS THAT WON'T STAND STILL

Fred and Ginger Frog never stand still. As Ballroom Dance Champions, they are always on the move!

These words are also on the move. Find the errors in spelling. Rewrite any misspelled words correctly on the line below the word.

scrammble

excape

carttwheel

climbbing

wigle

frolick

bounceing

slinkking

somersault

acrobatics

leeping

wobbel

wanderd

revolv

dancing **stumbleing**

shakeing **flieing** **craul**

bustle

twirreling

Name

40

WORDS THAT MAKE YOU LAUGH AND CRY

Some words make Frankie laugh. Others make him cry. Once he gets started laughing or crying, it's hard to get him to stop!

LAUGH

humor
joking
snicker
silliness
absurd
tickling
giggles
funniest
laughter
hilarious
comedy
amusement

Here are twelve words of each kind. They are all spelled correctly.

Choose 5 or more of the laughing words.
Use them in a short paragraph telling why he is laughing.
Make sure you spell the words right!

_____

_____

_____

_____

_____

_____

Choose 5 or more of the crying words.
Use them in a short paragraph telling why he is crying.
Make sure you spell the words right!

_____

_____

_____

_____

_____

_____

_____

CRY

injury
terror
insults
whine
sorrow
teasing
accident
loneliness
embarrass
dangerous
frightening
disappointment

Name _____

ITSY-BITSY WORDS

Words don't have to be big or complicated to cause spelling problems. Some of the most troublesome words are those small, short ones!

Little Miss Muffet Frog has spider trouble. She also has spelling trouble. Find all the mistakes and write those words correctly.

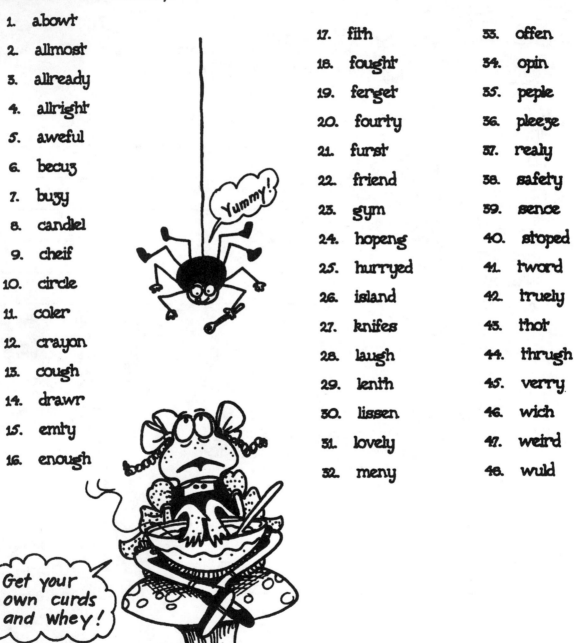

1. abowt
2. allmost
3. allready
4. allright
5. aweful
6. becuz
7. buzy
8. candlel
9. cheif
10. circle
11. coler
12. crayon
13. cough
14. drawr
15. emty
16. enough

17. filth
18. foughr
19. ferget
20. fourty
21. furst
22. friend
23. gym
24. hopeng
25. hurryed
26. island
27. knifes
28. laugh
29. lenth
30. lissen
31. lovely
32. meny

33. offen
34. opin
35. peple
36. pleeze
37. realy
38. safety
39. sence
40. stoped
41. tword
42. truely
43. thot
44. thrugh
45. verry
46. wich
47. weird
48. wuld

Get your own curds and whey!

Name

GIANT, COLOSSAL WORDS

Don't run away from big words. They're not as scary as the Abominable Snow-Frog. If you write one part at a time, they are not too hard to spell!

Find the FIVE words that are spelled wrong. Circle them.
Then, choose any TEN of these words and write a sentence that explains what the word is or what it means. Use a separate piece of paper.

Have no trepidation. I am not a monstrosity. Honest!

gymnasium
exaggerate
xylophone
civilization
videotape
caterpillar
abominable
biodegradable
monstrosity
bummblebee
encyclapedia
delicatessen
Pensylvannia
PHOTOSYNTHESIS
multiplacation

circumference
abracadabra
brontosaurus

butterscotch
electromagnetic
hippapotamus
orthodontist
perpendicular
precipitation
veterinarian

Name

WORDS WITH CHARACTER

How would you describe these characters? Would you use words like *extraordinary* . . .
hilarious . . . *terrifying* . . . *ridiculous?*

Look at the words in the box. Choose at least five to describe each character.
Write the words under the character. Make sure you spell them right!

admirable	curious	independent	serious
aggressive	delightful	merry	sneaky
agile	devious	mysterious	snooty
athletic	dreadful	nosy	stealthy
annoying	elegant	obnoxious	talented
clever	energetic	outrageous	tricky
comical	fancy	proper	troublesome
conceited	frightening	romantic	unusual

Name

UNEARTHLY WORDS

When Antonia Frog blasted off in the Amphibias 11 craft, she had no idea she would need her spelling dictionary. Help her get the right spellings for the words she encounters in outer space.

Finish the puzzle with words to fit the clues.

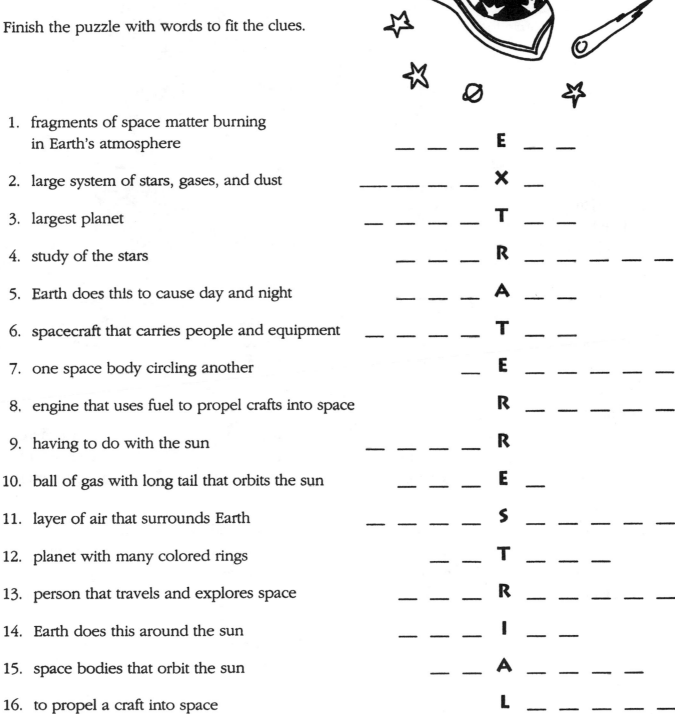

1. fragments of space matter burning in Earth's atmosphere   _ _ _ _ E _ _

2. large system of stars, gases, and dust   _ _ _ _ _ X _

3. largest planet   _ _ _ _ T _ _

4. study of the stars   _ _ _ R _ _ _ _ _

5. Earth does this to cause day and night   _ _ _ A _ _

6. spacecraft that carries people and equipment   _ _ _ _ T _ _

7. one space body circling another   _ E _ _ _ _ _

8. engine that uses fuel to propel crafts into space   R _ _ _ _ _

9. having to do with the sun   _ _ _ _ R

10. ball of gas with long tail that orbits the sun   _ _ _ E _

11. layer of air that surrounds Earth   _ _ _ _ S _ _ _ _ _

12. planet with many colored rings   _ _ T _ _ _

13. person that travels and explores space   _ _ _ R _ _ _ _

14. Earth does this around the sun   _ _ _ I _ _

15. space bodies that orbit the sun   _ _ _ A _ _ _ _

16. to propel a craft into space   L _ _ _ _ _

Name _____

WORDS THAT CONFUSE

Freddie is terribly confused about the spelling of these words. Maybe it's because these are some words that are spelled wrong very often. Help him out by deciding which spelling in each word group is correct. Circle the right one.

1. busness
   buziness
   business
   busyness

2. twelth
   twelvth
   twelfth
   twelveth

3. surprise
   suprize
   surprice
   surprise

4. cafateria
   cafetaria
   cafeteria
   cafeterria

5. calandar
   calendar
   calender
   calander

6. balloon
   baloon
   ballon
   baloone

7. embarrass
   embarass
   embbaras
   emmbarass

8. lisense
   lisence
   license
   licence

9. memary
   memory
   memry
   memmory

10. bannana
    bananna
    bannanna
    banana

11. memarise
    memorize
    memorise
    memmorize

12. nesessary
    nessessary
    necessary
    nessecary

13. Flordia
    Florida
    Floirda
    Floirida

14. restrant
    resturant
    restaurant
    restaurent

15. marshmellow
    marshmalow
    marshmallow
    marshmelow

16. reconize
    reconise
    recognize
    recognise

17. receive
    recieve
    resieve
    reseive

18. advertisement
    advertizment
    advertisment
    advertizement

19. trubble
    troubble
    troble
    trouble

20. vegtable
    vejetable
    veggetable
    vegetable

Name

46

WHO'S RIGHT?

Frannie and Frankie both studied for their spelling test. Who studied the hardest?
Look at both tests. Circle the numbers of the correctly-spelled words.

FRANKIE	FRANNIE
1. beried	1. buried
2. mystery	2. mistery
3. automatic	3. autamatic
4. neighbor	4. neighbor
5. Lincon	5. Lincoln
6. Tenessee	6. Tennessee
7. Wednesday	7. Wenesday
8. absence	8. absence
9. thorugh	9. thorough
10. jewelry	10. jewelry
11. somebody	11. sombody
12. chocalat	12. chocolate
13. radar	13. raydar
14. criticise	14. criticize
15. laughter	15. lafter
16. seperate	16. separate
17. fortunately	17. fortunately
18. enuf	18. enough
19. wheather	19. whether
20. practice	20. practise

A. Which speller did the best job on the test? _____

B. Which words were spelled correctly by both spellers? (List numbers.) _____

Name _____

SNIFFING OUT MISTAKES

Garth, the garbage collector, follows his nose to locate the garbage cans which need emptying. He is very good at deciding which ones have leftovers and other unwanted trash.

Which cans have unwanted misspelled words in them? Use your spelling sense to figure it out. Color the cans that have one or more misspelled words. Write the number of wrong words on the lid of each can (0–5).

#1.
rinkle
tangel
shoulder
shovell
quarter

#2.
porcupine
quantity
traffick
trophie
favrite

#3.
omitt
volume
walett
trapazoid
whistle

#4.
lazyest
eastren
terkey
reconize
lemin

#5.
faucet
confuse
difference
satisfy
regular

#6.
lable
legle
benafit
physicle
explain

peee-uoo!

GARBAGE

Name

SIGNS FOR SPELLERS

Freida is surprised by all the signs on the beach. For one thing, they are rather hard to read because of all the errors.

Fix the signs. Rewrite the message on each sign. Spell every word correctly!

49   *Basic Skills/Spelling 4-5*

HEADLINES IN NEED OF HELP

The newspaper editor fell asleep at his desk this morning, so no one got rid of the spelling errors. Edit these headlines. Write each one correctly in the space below the headline.

1. **BURGLER STEELS PRESIOUS PAINTINGS**

2. *VOLCANOE CAUZES TERIBBLE TRADGEDY*

3. *GIANT SLEEPS TWO HUNDERD YEARS*

4. ZOOKEEPER CHASES HIPOPOTOMOS TO MICHAGAN

5. **MAGIGIUN PULLS NINTY RABITTS FROM HAT**

6. *PELICAN RESKUES CHILD FROM SINKING YAHT*

7. **WRESSTLER WINS MILLYUN DOLLER PRISE**

8. **DOCTER DISKOVERS MIRACAL CURE FOR WARTS**

Name

APPENDIX

CONTENTS

10 SPELLING RULES

Rule 1: Write *i* before *e* except after *c*, or when sounded like *a*, as in *neighbor* or *weigh*. Some exceptions are: *their, height, foreign, heir, neither, weird,* and *seize*.

Rule 2: When a one-syllable word *(hit)* ends in a consonant *(t)* preceded by one vowel *(i)*, double the final consonant before adding a suffix which begins with a vowel *(ing; hitting)*.
When a multi-syllable word *(forget)* ends in a consonant *(t)* preceded by one vowel *(e)*, and the accent is on the last syllable *(for**GET**)*, and the suffix begins with a vowel *(ing)*—the same rule holds true: double the final consonant *(forgetting)*. *(swim-swimming; begin-beginning)*

Rule 3: If a word ends with a silent *e*, drop the *e* before adding a suffix which begins with a vowel *(use-using-useful; state-stating-statement; like-liking-likeness)*.
Note: Do not drop the *e* when the suffix begins with a consonant. Exceptions include *truly, argument,* and *ninth*.

Rule 4: When *y* is the last letter in a word and the *y* comes just after a vowel, add only s to make it plural *(boy-boys; tray-trays; monkey-monkeys)*.

Rule 5: The word ending pronounced *shun* is usually spelled *tion (conversation, motion, ration)*.

Rule 6: The spelling of a base word does not change when you add a prefix *(do-undo; work-rework; assemble-disassemble)*.

Rule 7: If the letter before a final *y* is a vowel, do not change the *y* when you add a suffix.
If the letter before a final *y* is a consonant, change the *y* to *i* before you add any suffix except *ing*. The *y* never changes before *ing*.

Rule 8: When the letters *c* and *g* have a hard sound, they are followed by *a, o,* or *u (organize, column, gusty)*.
When *c* and *g* have a soft sound, they are followed by the letters *i, e,* or *y (pencil, imagine, celery, legend, saucy, edgy)*. Suffixes that follow the soft *c* or *g* always begin with i or e *(ian, ion, ious, ence)*.

Rule 9: The letter *q* is always followed by the letter *u* in the English language.

Rule 10: The letters *gh* are silent in a few familiar letter combinations: *ough (ought), ight (tight), eigh (weigh)*.

SPELLER'S GUIDE TO CONFUSING SOUNDS

F   The *f* sound can be spelled with *f (funny, fantastic, friend)* or *ph (phone, physical, phrase)*.

G   The hard *g* sound can be spelled with *g (gate, gutter)* or with *gh (ghost, ghastly)*.

J   The *j* sound can be spelled with *j (jelly, jump)* or with *g (giant, gym, gem)*.

K   The *k* sound can be spelled with *k (kicking, kitchen)* or with *c (catsup, cantaloupe)* or with *ch (chorus, chemist)*.

N   The *n* sound can be spelled with *n (nifty, ninety)* or with *kn (knee, knot, knob)* or with *gn (gnat, gnome)* or with *pn (pneumonia)*.

R   The *r* sound can be spelled with *r (riddle, rascal)* or with *rh (rhinosceros, rhyme)* or with *wr (write, wriggle)*.

S   The *s* sound can be spelled with *s (Saturday, sassy)* or with *c (celery, city)* or with *sc (scissors, scene)* or with *psy (psychiatry)*.

T   The *t* sound can be spelled with *t (tickle, tackle)* or with *pt (pterodactyl)*.

W   The *w* sound can be spelled with *w (witch, wizard)* or with *wh (whine)*.

Z   The *z* sound can be spelled with *z (zero, zoo)* or with *x (xylophone)*.

KR   The *kr* sound can be spelled with *kr (krypton)* or with *cr (cranky, creepy)* or with *chr (Christmas)*.

SH   The *sh* sound can be spelled with *sh (shallow, shiver)* or with *ch (chef, chateau)* or with *s (sugar, sure)*.

SK   The *sk* sound can be spelled with *sk (skinny, skate)* or with *sc (scary, scrape)* or with *sch (scheme, school)* or with *squ (squirt, squeeze)*.

WORDS THAT ARE OFTEN MISSPELLED

absence	beginning	criticize	having
about	believe	curious	hear
accident	benefit	damage	heard
account	bicycle	deceive	height
accuse	biscuit	defense	here
ache	blue	delicious	history
achieve	brake	desert	hoarse
acre	break	diamond	honest
address	breakfast	difference	hour
advertise	breathe	disapprove	hundred
again	brief	doctor	hurried
aisle	built	does	icicle
allowance	burglar	done	immediately
almost	bury	don't	important
already	business	early	incident
always	busy	easy	initial
amateur	buy	embarrass	interrupt
ambulance	cafeteria	empty	interview
among	canal	enough	irregular
ancient	candle	every	island
angel	cannot	excellent	instead
animal	canoe	exercise	jealous
anniversary	can't	explain	journal
appear	carrot	extinct	journey
answer	carton	February	juice
any	caught	Florida	just
athlete	certain	forget	justice
August	character	forty	kitchen
baking	chief	fountain	knead
balloon	chocolate	fourth	knew
banana	choose	fragile	knife
beauty	chorus	frequent	knives
beautiful	circle	friend	knock
because	climb	frighten	know
been	cocoa	gauge	laboratory
	collar	genius	laid
	color	ghost	language
	Columbus	gorgeous	laugh
	coming	graduate	lawyer
	committee	grammar	league
	cough	grief	lemon
	could	guarantee	length
	country	guess	library
	courage	hamburger	license

lightning	opposite	require	two
likable	ordinary	reservoir	typical
likeness	original	resign	umbrella
Lincoln	ought	restaurant	uniform
listen	oxygen	rhyme	unique
literature	pajamas	ridiculous	universe
location	particle	said	unusual
loose	paid	safety	useable
lose	parallel	sandwich	used
lovely	patient	says	usually
machinery	peculiar	scene	vacuum
magnify	people	scissors	vegetable
making	perform	seize	very
manageable	physician	separate	virus
many	picnic	shoes	visible
marriage	piece	since	voice
marshmallow	pilot	sincere	wear
meant	pleasant	sleigh	weather
measurement	please	society	Wednesday
medal	pleasure	some	week
medium	pledge	somebody	weigh
memorize	police	stalk	where
minute	practice	stopped	whether
molecule	precious	straight	which
mosquito	presence	sugar	whistle
movement	prize	sure	whoever
much	program	taught	whole
mystery	quantity	tear	women
national	quarrel	terrible	won't
naughty	quarter	terrific	would
necessary	question	their	wreath
neighbor	quiet	they	write
neither	quite	thorough	writhe
ninety	rabbit	though	writing
none	raise	through	wrote
notice	read	tired	yacht
noticeable	ready	tomorrow	yellow
nuclear	realize	tonight	your
numb	really	tongue	you're
obey	receive	too	
occasionally	recent	toward	
occur	recognize	triangle	
official	refer	trouble	
often	rehearse	truly	
once	reign	Tuesday	
opaque	remedy	twelfth	

SPELLING
SKILLS TEST

Fill in *ie* or *ei* for each word.

1. bel _____ ve
2. n _____ ghbor
3. fr _____ nd
4. rec _____ ve
5. w _____ ght
6. ach _____ ve

Write the correct ending for each word.

7. nerv _____ (ous, eous, ious)
8. pleas _____ (ent, int, ant)
9. imposs _____ (able, ible, ibel)
10. rad _____ (ous, ious, ius, us)
11. compl _____ (eat, ete, ate)
12. trav _____ (al, el, il, le)
13. import _____ (ence, ince, ance)
14. vaca _____ (cian, shun, tion, sion)
15. carniv _____ (al, el, il, le)
16. chocol _____ (ete, ate, eat)

Which words on Freddy's poster do NOT have silent letters? Write them below.

stalk	bridge
ghost	honest
envy	sword
combing	erupt
wriggle	knife

shhhhh

17. _____

Which words on Pierre's poster are NOT correct? Write them on the lines correctly.

firecracker   celery   enerjy

couffed   surprice   phone

skuba   sider   babisitter

18. _____
19. _____
20. _____
21. _____
22. _____
23. _____

Are these words spelled correctly? Write yes or no next to each word.

_____ 24. tommorrow

_____ 25. Tennessee

_____ 26. memmory

_____ 27. bannana

_____ 28. terrible

_____ 29. annimal

_____ 30. syllable

Name _____

Write each word in its plural form.

31. radio   _____

32. monkey   _____

33. loaf   _____

34. mess   _____

35. butterfly   _____

36. goose   _____

Write each word in its PAST tense.

37. worry   _____

38. wish   _____

39. argue   _____

40. freeze   _____

41. forget   _____

Circle the correctly-spelled word in each group.

42. Atlantic, Antartica, Brasil

43. Lincon, Warshington, Jupiter

44. Checago, Michigan, Las Angelas

45. Wednesday, Tuseday, Saterday

46. Chrissmas, Haloween, Thanksgiving

Circle the word in each group that is NOT spelled correctly.

47. tomatoes
torpedoes
pianoes
volcanoes
solos

48. wierd
ancient
their
height
beige

49. homework
bookkeeper
roommate
notbook
somebody

50. completely
magecal
favorable
accidental
dentist

51. subbmarine
transport
exclude
semicircle
antiwar

52. terrifick
agreement
dangerous
explosion
tropical

53. arithmatic
caterpillar
Pennsylvania
hippopotamus

54. stubborn
elegent
comical
curious

55. galaxy
astronot
rotation
atmosphere

Name _____

Which words on the chef's shopping list are spelled INCORRECTLY? Write them correctly below.

SHOPPING LIST

vegtables
custard
suger
macaroni
spaghetti
chocolate
lettuse
onions
sausage
tomatos
noodels

56. _____

_____

These words are all misspelled. Write them correctly.

57. pilat _____
58. peopel _____
59. cought _____
60. molacule _____
61. lama _____
62. lafter _____
63. agin _____
64. appeer _____
65. enugh _____

Which word is spelled correctly? Circle the correct spelling.

66. separate, seperate
67. absence, abcense
68. criticize, criticise
69. wheather, weather
70. autamatic, automatic
71. license, lisence

Write these misspelled words correctly.

72. toung _____
73. mosquitoe _____
74. oder _____
75. oppisite _____
76. lonleyness _____
77. lenth _____
78. pleeze _____
79. allmost _____
80. nesessary _____

81. **Circle the correctly-spelled words on Sheriff Frog's poster.**

WANTED

wieght   wreath   wisper
expel   tragady   seize
apologize   wepons   satasfy
prise   oxygen   serious
rhithm   exercize   excellent
quisses   stomack   quartet
strength   explane   gravity
squeaze   zero   buzy

Name _____

Circle the correct spelling of each of these confusing words.

82. suprice   surprize   surprise
83. baloon   balloon   ballon
84. marshmellow   marshmalow   marshmallow
85. calender   calendar   callendar

Write the correct word to finish each sentence.

86. _____ (Adopt, Adept) a pet today!

87. I _____ (except, accept) your apology.

88. Count the _____ (angels, angles) in your rectangle.

89. Did you do a _____ (through, though, thorough) job of cleaning?

90. I write in my _____ (dairy, diary) every day.

91. For breakfast, I ate bran _____ (cereal, serial) today.

92. My library book has been _____ (overdue, overdo) for a week.

93. My cat actually _____ (pried, pride) open the cat food box!

94. My _____ (hoarse, horse) is too old to ride anymore.

95. Don't _____ (break, brake) any bones!

Re-write each headline, spelling all the words correctly.

96. FRIEK AXIDENTS REPORTTED ON PUBLIK BEECHES

96. _____

97. DOCTER DOES SUPRIZE OPARATION

97. _____

98. SKI SESON CANCELLED DUE TO DANGROUS ICE STORM

98. _____

99. TWO HUNRERD HOMES LOST IN TORNADOE

99. _____

100. ELAPHANT RECIEVES GOLD MEDDLE

100. _____

Total Score _____ out of 100 points.

Name

ANSWER KEY

SKILLS TEST

1. ie
2. ei
3. ie
4. ei
5. ei
6. ie
7. ous
8. ant
9. ible
10. ius
11. ete
12. el
13. ance
14. tion
15. al
16. ate
17. erupt
18–23. energy, coughed, surprise, scuba, cider, babysitter
24. no
25. yes
26. no
27. no
28. yes
29. no
30. yes
31. radios
32. monkeys
33. loaves
34. messes
35. butterflies
36. geese
37. worried
38. wished
39. argued
40. froze
41. forgot
42. Atlantic
43. Jupiter
44. Michigan
45. Wednesday
46. Thanksgiving
47. pianoes
48. wierd
49. notbook
50. magecal
51. subbmarine
52. terrifick
53. arithmatic
54. elegent
55. astronot
56. vegetables, sugar, lettuce, tomatoes, noodles

57. pilot
58. people
59. caught
60. molecule
61. llama
62. laughter
63. again
64. appear
65. enough
66. separate
67. absence
68. criticize
69. weather
70. automatic
71. license
72. tongue
73. mosquito
74. odor
75. opposite
76. loneliness
77. length
78. please
79. almost
80. necessary
81. Circle: wreath, expel, seize, apologize, oxygen, serious, excellent, quartet, strength, gravity, zero
82. surprise
83. balloon
84. marshmallow
85. calendar
86. Adopt
87. accept
88. angles
89. thorough
90. diary
91. cereal
92. overdue
93. pried
94. horse
95. break
96. Freak Accidents Reported On Public Beaches
97. Doctor Does Surprise Operation
98. Ski Season Canceled Due To Dangerous Ice Storm
99. Two Hundred Homes Lost in Tornado
100. Elephant Receives Gold Medal

SKILLS EXERCISES

Page 10

These words should be circled:
  tommorrow
  vollunteer
  bennefit
  memmory
  proffessor
  annimal
  attenndance
  baskettball
  catterpillar
  bannana
  tellescope

Page 11

1. a
2. b
3. b
4. b
5. a
6. a
7. a
8. a
9. a
10. b
11. a
12. b
13. a
14. a
15. a
16. b
17. a
18. b

Page 12

Correct words that should be colored:
1. hitchhiker
2. lighthouse
3. nightmare
4. nighttime
5. countryside
6. grandmother
7. wheelchair
8. floodlight
10. sandpaper
12. headache
16. greenhouse
17. heartbreak
18. quicksand
22. seaside

Page 13

Incorrect words to be circled and re-spelled correctly:

Friday, June 13: circus, laughing, celery, emergency, coughed

Saturday, June 14: phone, phony, judge, citizenship, ridiculous

Sunday, June 15: ghastly, ghosts, celebration, mischief, cider

Monday, June 16: physical, certainly, energized, surprised, photographs

Tuesday, June 17: caught, cyclone, patience, scuba

Page 14

1. children
2. noises
3. messes
4. wishes
5. societies
6. cottages
7. addresses
8. chefs
9. butterflies
10. heroes
11. loaves
12. chiefs
13. geese
14. echoes
15. donkeys
16. women
17. radios
18. keys
19. potatoes
20. athletes
21. lunches
22. foxes
23. counties
24. nests
25. attorneys

Page 15

1. Egypt
2. North Atlantic Ocean
3. Los Angeles
4. The Eiffel Tower
5. Interstate 80
6. Queen Elizabeth's Kitchen
7. The Golden Gate Bridge
8. Detroit, Michigan
9. Jupiter
10. Mount Rushmore
11. Washington D.C.
12. The Philippines
13. The Statue of Liberty
14. The Amazon River

15. Antarctica
16. Rhode Island
17. South America
18. Paris, France
19. Australia
20. Brazil

Page 16

1. fought
2. argued
3. giggled
4. required
5. chose
6. polished
7. brought
8. worried
9. got
10. married
11. froze
12. shone
13. rusted; forgot
14. tried
15. wished

Page 17

1. ite
2. ive
3. ise
4. ish
5. ish
6. ize
7. ish
8. ise
9. ive
10. ist
11. ile
12. ize
13. ish
14. age
15. ege or age
16. edge
17. age
18. ist
19. age
20. age

Page 18

1. jealous
2. circus
3. focus
4. tremendous
5. melodious
6. generous
7. marvelous
8. conscious
9. cautious
10. radius
11. outrageous
12. luscious
13. Venus
14. nervous
15. cactus

Page 19

1. distant
2. evident
3. hydrant
4. independent
5. pleasant
6. elegant
7. vacant
8. excitement
9. ignorant
10. importance
11. appliance
12. elephant
13. restaurant
14. science
15. absence
16. insurance
17. attendance
18. evidence

Page 20

1. impossible
2. legal
3. quarrel
4. vacation
5. musician
6. visible
7. adorable
8. cushion
9. carnival
10. fatal
11. magician
12. icicle
13. prevention
14. candle
15. cancel
16. tradition
17. channel
18. travel
19. cancel
20. reversible

Page 21

1. ate
2. ate
3. ate
4. eat
5. ate
6. ate
7. ete
8. ate
9. ite
10. ate
11. ate
12. eat
13. ate
14. ate
15. ete
16. ate
17. ate
18. ite

Page 22

Rule # 1
Circle: pianos, solos

Rule # 2
Circle: weird, ancient, neither, height, foreign

Rule # 3
Circle: pastime

Rule # 4
Circle: wholly, truly

Rule # 5
Circle: noticeable, manageable

Page 23

Misspelled words are:
1. supernatural
5. completely
6. feverish
10. biography
11. magical
12. disappear
13. preschool
16. musical
20. advertisement

Page 24

1. submarine
2. microphone
3. extraordinary
4. rewrite
5. unicycle
6. hexagon
7. impossible
8. international
9. mislabel
10. transport
11. exclude
12. pregame
13. postholiday
14. antibacterial
15. semicircle
16. unfriendly

Page 25

Words spelled correctly are:
tragic
scary
generally
completely
explosion
terrific
agreement
hardship
disappointment
different
actor
dangerous

Page 26

Words with no silent letters are:

envy, burglar, bumpy, quiver, automatic, erupt, coconut

Page 27

1. unique
2. inquire
3. conquer
4. squash
5. banquet
6. equator
7. quickly
8. quiet
9. sequel
10. quilt
11. quartet
12. quizzes
13. aquarium
14. quarrel
15. frequently
16. question
17. equipment

Page 28

Words spelled correctly are:
1. slippery
6. soccer
8. stomach
11. suspect
14. serious
15. stereo
22. seventh
23. strengthen
24. scissors
25. hissing
26. surely
27. successful
29. special
30. seize
31. squirm
32. studio

Page 29

William Weightlifter
Wretched Ray
Worst Woodpecker
Weird Wanda Worm
Wrestler Rachel
Weekend Warrior
1. awful
2. wasteful
3. windowsill
4. weight
5. wonderful
6. weapons
7. which or witch
8. we're
9. knowledge

10. wreath
11. whisper
12. wrapping
13. whipped or wiped
14. Wednesday
15. wrinkled
16. weakness

Page 30

1. expel
2. saxophone
3. extinct
4. Mexico
5. flex
6. excellent
7. examine
8. exist
9. hexagon
10. maximum
11. exclaim
12. exciting
13. next
14. foxes
15. extreme
16. oxygen
17. excuse
18. exercise
19. exterior
20. flexible
21. mixture
22. exit
23. expect
24. explode
25. expressway

Page 31

1. yummy
2. envy
3. magnify
4. rhythm
5. yolk
6. rhyme
7. guilty
8. yesterday
9. gravity
10. hyphen
11. chewy
12. synonym
13. oxygen
14. yogurt
15. mystery

Page 32

Across
1. prize
3. zipper
5. buzz
7. apologize
9. freezer
11. zero
13. blizzard
16. fizzle

17. jazz
18. cozy
DOWN
2. organize
4. squeeze
6. hazard
8. dozen
10. realize
12. lazy
14. dizzy
15. fizzy

Page 33

Words to be corrected:
(correct spelling)
2. carrot
4. pilot
5. molecule
6. volcano
8. doctor
9. opposite
12. memory
13. gorilla (or guerrilla)
12. octopus
13. October
15. scorpion
16. cocoon
18. mosquito
19. abdomen
20. dinosaur
23. odor

Page 34

1. ea
2. ou
3. ai
4. ui or ai
5. ou
6. au
7. ai
8. ou
9. ea
10. oi
11. ue
12. ai
13. eo
14. ie
15. ou
16. au
17. ea
18. ua
19. au
20. au

Page 35

Correct words to be circled:
bizarre
unique
kazoo
scheme
opaque

gnome
karate
bough
enough
karate
vague
amnesia
Incorrect words (corrected):
Des Moines
Connecticut
llama
tongue
vacuum
bronchitis
mustache
pneumonia
zigzag

Page 36

Correct phrases:
adopt a pet
Eat your celery!
That's no excuse!
cute cartoons on TV
a custard pie
an inspiring story
I accept your present.
walking on crutches
Write in your diary.
my red and white
striped socks
art hanging in galleries

Page 37

1. pried
2. creaky
3. wait, medal
4. throne, reigned
5. sent, chews
6. freeze, tails
7. aunt's, raise
8. overdue, week
9. hoarse
10. whoop, scent
11. cereal, Claus
12. Pedal, rung
13. fleas, hair

Page 38

1. spaghetti
2. doughnut or donut
3. mosquito
4. kindergarten
5. yacht
6. pajamas
7. pirate
8. octopus
9. umbrella
10. shampoo
11. vanilla
12. comet
13. lasso

14. piano
15. antique
16. dynamite
17. diamond
18. tornado

Page 39

Menus 4 and 7 have all words spelled correctly.
Menu #1: 2 mistakes—vegetable, molasses
Menu #2: 3 mistakes—appetizers, coconut, crumb
Menu #3: 5 mistakes—cranberries, spinach, salad, sugar, broccoli
Menu #5: 5 mistakes—pasta, lamb, celery, pineapple, bologna
Menu #6: 1 mistake—radishes
Menu #8: 6 mistakes—cheese, biscuits, apricot, chocolate, sundae, banana

Page 40

Words spelled wrong:
wiggle
wobble
stumbling
crawl
revolve
slinking
frolic
cartwheel
scramble
bouncing
escape
climbing
flying
leaping
wandered
twirling
shaking

Page 41

Sentences will vary. Check to see that the words found on this page are spelled correctly in student's writing.

Page 42

Incorrect words to be corrected:
1. about
2. almost
3. already
4. alright or all right
5. awful
6. because
7. busy
8. candle
9. chief
11. color
14. drawer
15. empty
17. fifth

19. forget
20. forty
21. first
24. hoping
25. hurried
27. knives
29. length
30. listen
32. many
33. often
34. open
35. people
36. please
37. really
39. since or sense or cents
40. stopped or stooped
41. toward
42. truly
43. thought
44. through
45. very
46. which or witch
48. would

Page 43

Words spelled wrong:
multiplication
Pennsylvania
hippopotamus
encyclopedia
bumblebee
Student choices and definitions will vary. Check to make sure that students have spelled the big words correctly.

Page 44

Answers will vary. Make sure that students use correct spelling for the words they choose to describe each character.

Page 45

1. meteor
2. galaxy
3. Jupiter
4. astronomy
5. rotate
6. shuttle
7. revolve
8. rocket
9. solar
10. comet
11. atmosphere
12. Saturn
13. astronaut
14. orbits
15. planets
16. launch

Page 46

1. business or busyness
2. twelfth
3. surprise

4. cafeteria
5. calendar
6. balloon
7. embarrass
8. license
9. memory
10. banana
11. memorize
12. necessary
13. Florida
14. restaurant
15. marshmallow
16. recognize
17. receive
18. advertisement
19. trouble
20. vegetable

Page 47

Frannie has these correct: 1, 4, 5, 6, 8, 9, 10, 12, 14, 16, 17, 18, 19
Frankie has these correct: 2, 3, 4, 7, 8, 10, 11, 13, 15, 17, 20
A. Frannie
B. words # 4, 8, 10, 17

Page 48

Cans that should be colored:
  #1, #2, #3, #4, #6,
1. 3 mistakes
2. 3 mistakes
3. 3 mistakes
4. 5 mistakes
5. 0 mistakes
6. 4 mistakes

Page 49

1. Report All Accidents Immediately
2. No Horses Allowed on Beach
3. Marshmallow Roasting on Wednesdays Only
4. Public Beach No Lifeguard
5. Summer is Canceled Until Further Notice
6. No Swimming to the Island
7. Beware! Dangerous Sea Animals
8. Life Preservers Required on Boats
9. Water is Occupied by Sea Monsters

Page 50

1. Burglar Steals Precious Paintings
2. Volcano Causes Terrible Tragedy
3. Giant Sleeps Two Hundred Years
4. Zookeeper Chases Hippopotamus to Michigan
5. Magician Pulls Ninety Rabbits From Hat
6. Pelican Rescues Child From Sinking Yacht
7. Wrestler Wins Million Dollar Prize
8. Doctor Discovers Miracle Cure for Warts